# THE
# POCKET

# ROCKY
# HORROR

**G:**

Published in 2025
by Gemini Gift Books
Part of Gemini Books Group

Based in Woodbridge and London

Marine House, Tide Mill Way,
Woodbridge, Suffolk IP12 1AP
United Kingdom
www.geminibooks.com

Text and Design © 2025 Gemini Gift Books Ltd

Part of the Gemini Pockets series

Cover illustration by Natalie Foss

ISBN 978-1-80247-324-7

Manufacturer's EU Representative: Eurolink Compliance Limited, 25 Herbert Place, Dublin, D02 AY86, Republic of Ireland. admin@eurolink-europe.ie

Printed in China

10 9 8 7 6 5 4 3 2 1

# THE POCKET

# ROCKY HORROR

G:

# CONTENTS

———•———

# "I would like, if I may, to take you on a strange journey..."

With these iconic words from the film's narrator, *The Rocky Horror Picture Show* began with a BANG... and then a flat tyre.

From that moment, the world was never the same again. Especially for Brad and Janet. But, dammit, we'll get to that.

# INTRODUCTION

Written in the very early 1970s by unemployed actor – and now British national treasure – Richard O'Brien, the *Rocky Horror Show* began life as a gender-bending, time-warping, cross-dressing madcap theatre musical homage to American sci-fi B-movies... via Mary Shelley's 1818 literary masterpiece, *Frankenstein*. Yes, it's as every bit as ridiculous as that sentence sounds. The show was such a hit that within 18 months a movie adaptation – *The Rocky Horror Picture Show* – was birthed with the same creative juices.

A camp masterpiece, and the ultimate cult movie, *The Rocky Horror Picture Show* remains an icon of modern cinema.

This *Pocket Rocky Horror* motorcycles down Memory Lane to celebrate a movie so relentlessly brilliant and bonkers that, naturally, we can't live without it. So, if you're ready, let's do the time warp again. Just remember: Enter at your own risk.

# CHAPTER ONE

# HAPPY BIRTHDAY ROCKY

# GIVE YOURSELF OVER TO ABSOLUTE PLEASURE!

# BLOOD RED LIPS EMERGE FROM THE VOID, AND SING

The iconic lips that emerge at the start of the film belong to Patricia Quinn, who plays Magenta, Riff-Raff's sister and Dr Frank's maid at Frankenstein Place. While Patricia's lips move to sing the opening number 'Science Fiction/Double Feature', the song is actually sung by *Rocky Horror* creator, Richard O'Brien. Patricia was furious when she found out she wasn't singing the song as she had in the theatre production. "You BASTARD! You took my song!" she screamed. "Those lips have outdone Jagger, they're the most famous lips in the world," she told *Sci-Fi Now* (July 2019).

# MAIN CAST

Dr Frank-N-Furter – **Tim Curry**

Riff-Raff – **Richard O'Brien**

Janet Weiss – **Susan Sarandon**

Brad Majors – **Barry Bostwick**

Magenta – **Patricia Quinn**

Columbia – **Nell Campbell**

Dr Everett Von Scott – **Jonathan Adams**

The Criminologist – **Charles Gray**

Rocky – **Pete Hinwood**

Eddie – **Meat Loaf**

In 2025, we celebrate the film's 50th birthday – and marvel how this cult classic catapulted many of its cast to stardom, and has become a beacon of pride for the LGBTQIA+ and drag communities.

Dr Frank-N-Furter's message of "Don't dream it, be it!" resonates with fans in every generation since.

Prudish society at the time of its release may have been horrified by the film's "mental mind fuck", but all that proved was how ahead of its time it was.

# PLOT RECAP

*The plot of both the theatre show and the movie is famously shambolic, so let's do a quick refresher...*

The story follows a newly engaged couple, Brad and Janet, who's car suddenly blows a tyre during a storm. They see a light on at a mysterious castle, called Frankenstein Place, owned by the eccentric Dr Frank-N-Furter, and seek refuge there. They are welcomed by the eerie servants Riff-Raff, Magenta and Columbia, who lead them in to the ballroom where the "Transylvanian Annual Convention" (a bunch of aliens) are having a party. The gathered throng dance to the 'Time Warp'.

After, the flamboyant Dr Frank-N-Furter makes an entrance and introduces himself through song as a "Sweet transvestite from Transsexual, Transylvania". Dr Frank is keen to show Brad and Janet his "experimental creation" — a muscular man he has created to be his sex toy.

Out of nowhere, Eddie — an ex-delivery boy former lover of Columbia and test subject of Dr Frank — bursts out of a freezer and performs 'Hot Patootie'. Dr Frank quickly bludgeons him to death with a pickaxe.

*Breathe.*

Next, Dr Frank seduces Brad and Janet separately – by dressing up as them! – leading a horrified Janet to have sex with Rocky. Afterwards, the guests have dinner and unknowingly eat a meal made from Eddie's corpse. Frank then reveals the source of their meal, and forces the horrified Brad and Janet to perform a floor show in corsets and lingerie, culminating in an extravagant performance of 'Don't Dream It, Be It'.

For the finale, Riff-Raff and Magenta then reveal their plan to return to their home planet, Transsexual, and kill Frank for his monstrous behaviour. The pair then take off in the castle/spaceship, leaving Brad and Janet to crawl away in shock. The film ends with the song 'Super Heroes' as the survivors reflect on their bizarre night at the castle. All caught up?

# 14 AUGUST 1975

The original UK release date and premiere of *The Rocky Horror Picture Show* at the Rialto Theatre, London. The film was premiered in the US on 26 September at the UA Westwood in Los Angeles. The film cost £1.4 million to produce and two months to shoot. It flopped. BUT... WAIT! ...

As of 2025, *The Rocky Horror Picture Show* has grossed more than US $630 million worldwide (adjusted for inflation), and holds the Guinness World Record of longest-running theatrical release of any film. It's being playing in theatres, now predominantly over Halloween, all over the world for 50 years!

The Oriental Theatre, Milwaukee, Wisconsin is the longest continuously running location for showing the movie, with its first weekly showing on 7 January... 1978!

# SHOCK TREATMENT

Directed by Jim Sharman, and co-written by Sharman and Richard O'Brien, *Shock Treatment* is the pseudo-sequel movie to *The Rocky Horror Picture Show*. The plot focuses on Brad and Janet's lives after they return to Denton following their misadventures in *Rocky Horror*. The film rarely sees the light of day today, and was a critical and commercial failure – but well worth a watch! "It is a completely flawed movie but it has its saving graces," Richard O'Brien told *Pink News* in November 2011. "I think the score is better than *Rocky* and there are some pretty witty lyrics in there." Have you seen it?

# "A mental mind fuck can be nice."

**Dr Frank-N-Furter,** *The Rocky Horror Picture Show,* **1975**

# 2,600

The number of performances – a Guinness World Record – Welsh actor, Kristian Lavercombe, has performed as Riff-Raff since 2010 for scores of nationwide, international and world tours, including the 50th anniversary world tour. He's been described by Richard O'Brien as "a fantastically talented Riff-Raff".

"I can't really imagine my life without *Rocky*," the actor told the BBC in May 2023, "... it's still a relevant show and is going from strength to strength. *Rocky Horror* audiences are the best... they do all the things you wouldn't normally do at a theatre... it's preaching a sentiment that is very popular with audiences, which is to be yourself."

# A WICKED SMILE

In March 2005, Tim Curry appeared on Terry Gross's Fresh Air radio show and revealed a secret that made headlines around the world. While Tim was performing in a National Theatre production of *Love for Love* in 1986, one night Prince Charles and Princess Diana met with actors from the show. When Princess Diana saw Tim, she revealed that she loved *The Rocky Horror Picture Show*. "With a wicked smile," Tim said, "the Princess told me that the movie 'quite completed my education'." The royal seal of approval, indeed. Tim Curry's accent in the movie is, in fact, based on Queen Elizabeth II.

# GOING GAGA

In 50 years, *The Rocky Horror Picture Show* has picked up not just a famously dedicated cult following, it also has a wealth of famous fans too. Lady Gaga has cited the movie as a major influence on her music and fashion. The director Tim Burton has claimed his obsession with gothic and camp style developed from his love of *Rocky Horror*. Queen's Freddie Mercury loved the stage version and film, and became good friends with Tim Curry. Quentin Tarantino is a huge fan too, claiming *Rocky Horror* inspired his midnight-movie aesthetic. Outside of Prince and Madonna (both huge fans), probably the most famous stan of the movie remains Jack Black. "It's fucking crazy that we still live in this world, but it just goes to show you the power of *Rocky Horror* is still as relevant and necessary as ever right now," he has said.

"Writing *Rocky* was almost like working on a jigsaw puzzle. I had written several of the songs before and all I had to do was slot them in. I didn't start at the beginning and develop the plot from there. I started at both ends and then filled in the middle."

**Richard O'Brien, *Rocky Horror Picture Show Official Magazine* 1979**

# RICHARD O'BRIEN

A beloved British national treasure, *Rocky Horror* creator Richard O'Brien has been a familiar face on British television, film and stage since *Rocky* blew the bloody doors off the Royal Court Theatre in 1973. Richard also found fame elsewhere starring in 1980's *Flash Gordon* and the 1990s *The Crystal Maze*, a game show that has since achieved immortality on British TV. "*The Rocky Horror Show* has opened a lot of doors for me," Richard said. "But despite my so-called success, I guess I still see myself as an actor who is temporarily unemployed."

"Give yourself over to absolute pleasure. Swim the warm waters of sins of the flesh – erotic nightmares beyond any measure, and sensual daydreams to treasure forever. Can't you just see it? Don't dream it, be it."

Dr Frank-N-Furter, *The Rocky Horror Picture Show*, 1975

# 2,960

The incredible number of performances *Rocky Horror*'s original West End show ran for in London from 1973 to 1980. "*Rocky* never fails to deliver," Richard O'Brien said of his own monstrous creation to an audience in Norwich Theatre, August 2023. "Each performance lifts the heart and the nightly laughter and roars of approval leave the whole cast with a sense of wellbeing and accomplishment that you rarely get from any other shows."

* The first American performance of the stage show took place at the Roxy Theatre, Los Angeles, California, in March 1974 and ran for nine months.

# CROWE'S DEBUT

In a weird turn as unexpected as many of the plot twists in *Rocky Horror*, we're pleased to share with you the fact that Hollywood legend, Russell Crowe's first ever professional acting job was playing Eddie on stage.

For two years, from 1986 to 1988, Russell – billed as Russ le Roq – toured his homeland as part of the national Australian tour. "I did 458 performances," he told *Interview* magazine in 1997. "I was Eddie and Dr Scott for about 400 performances and about 58 as Frank-N-Furter. It's the only show that kept my interest, and that's because it changed every night because of the audience reaction."

Russell found worldwide fame in *Romper Stomper* in 1992.

# "If only we were amongst friends... or sane persons!"

Janet Weiss, *The Rocky Horror Picture Show,* 1975

# ON YOUR FEET!

Thanks to the legacy, and lunacy, of its worldwide cult following, *The Rocky Horror Picture Show* has set a few firsts in modern cinema history. It is the first film that received, and encouraged, audience participation; the first to have regular midnight screenings, starting in 1976; the first film adapted from a British stage musical to gain a cult legacy; and the first openly gender-fluid and LGBTQIA+-embracing mainstream musical film. It was also the first feature film to encourage – nay, demand! – cosplay, influencing conventions and fan events several years before other more mainstream films took the credit.

"All I wanted to do was play Eddie, pop out of a Coke machine, sing a rock'n'roll song, and pop back into the Coke machine. I was really nervous about the whole thing. But I respected Jim Sharman and since he felt I should play Riff-Raff I had to go along with him."

**Richard O'Brien, *Rocky Horror Picture Show Official Magazine* 1979**

"For a lot of people, *Rocky Horror* is their home, it's their connection to everybody – all their friends. I know of a lot of people whose lives were saved by this movie. Especially for those in the LGBT community, it's a place where they could be themselves and find people who were their family. I don't want to give that up. I want people to still have a place to be."

Larry Viezel, President of *The Rocky Horror Picture Show* Official Fan Club, BBC, June 2020

"Originally I played Frank-N-Furter as though he was German. ... Then, one day I heard a woman on a bus saying, 'Do you have a hise [house] in town or a hise [house] in the country?' And I thought, yes he should sound like the Queen. So that's how that happened."

**Tim Curry, *NPR*, March 2005**

# "And now, Frank-N-Furter, your time has come. Say good-bye to all of this... and hello to oblivion."

**Riff Raff, *The Rocky Horror Picture Show*, 1975**

"Hi! My name is Brad Majors, and this is my fiancée, Janet Weiss. I wonder if you might help us. You see, our car broke down a few miles up the road. Do you have a phone we might use?"

Brad Majors, *The Rocky Horror Picture Show*, 1975

# BRAD MAJORS

Now a famous TV actor, Barry Bostwick took on the role of Brad Majors in 1974, as one of the two Americans cast for the movie (the other was Susan Sarandon). Barry's performance as college student, and "hero", Brad is perfection – in particular, the uttering of the movie's most immortal line, "Dammit, Janet!", a quote that comes from the second number of the same name. For the first 30 minutes of the film, Brad and Janet are soaking wet. "They were always saying between each scene, 'Wet them down'. Then some ghoul with a spray gun would come by and have this smile on her face as they turned on the power and sprayed us with water. It was 20 degrees out. It was a hard shoot."

# *Frankenstein*

Richard O'Brien's vision for the stage show and movie was – very loosely – based on Mary Shelley's 1818 masterpiece, *Frankenstein*; itself a tale that blends horror, sci-fi and a large dollop of campness. The book's origins are as thrilling as the novel itself.

In 1816, 18-year-old Mary Shelley, Percy Bysshe Shelley, Lord Byron, and John Polidori rented Villa Diodati on Lake Geneva, during the "Year Without a Summer". Byron proposed a ghost story competition, inspiring Mary to conceive *Frankenstein* after she had a vivid waking nightmare of a scientist reanimating a corpse.

"It was funny when we were making it, I thought we were sort of making a contemporary *Sound of Music*."

**Barry Bostwick,
*L.A. Times*, October 1995**

# "NO, DON'T DO IT!"

This immortal line was the first ever shout-out of audience participation during the *Rocky Horror Show*'s first theatrical run in 1973 at the 63-seat Royal Court Theatre, London. According to Tim Curry, it was David Bowie's* first wife, Angie, who yelled "No, don't do it!" when Riff-Raff threatened to zap Tim Curry's Dr Frank-N-Furter with a laser gun.

*Bowie also passed on the role of Frank-N-Furter during the stage show's production.

# SIGNIFICANT

Perhaps the biggest honour ever bestowed on *The Rocky Horror Picture Show* was in 2005 when the movie was deemed "culturally, historically or aesthetically significant" and added to the Library of Congress' National Film Registry, alongside *The Sting* and *Toy Story*.

The registry summed the film up perfectly, and even quoted the 'Time Warp':

"The ultimate midnight movie, *Rocky Horror* revolutionized prevailing notions of audience participation during film screenings. Words to remember: 'It's astounding, time is fleeting, madness takes its toll.'"

# "I'm just a sweet transvestite from Transsexual, Transylvania."

**Dr Frank-N-Furter,** *The Rocky Horror Picture Show,* **1975**

# TIM CURRY

Following his legendary breakout role in *The Rocky Horror Picture Show*, his first feature film, the then unknown-actor Tim Curry (Dr Frank-N-Furter) was quick to become an international star of stage and screen. He has starred in many blockbuster films, including *Annie* (1982), *Clue* (1985), *The Hunt for Red October* (1990) and *The Three Musketeers* (1993). His powerful performances and distinctive voice made him a sought-after villain, most notably as Pennywise, the murderous clown in *It* (1990).

# "It was only meant to run for three weeks! Now it's 50 years old!"

**Richard O'Brien, *Guardian*, November 2022**

# CHAPTER TWO

## A RATHER TENDER SUBJECT

The movie's message of acceptance
– it's OK to be different – has ensured
its relevance and resonance with
movie-goers of several generations
since its 1975 release.

The film's moral lessons – or Aesop's,
as they are known, after Aesop's
Fables – relate to the outrageous
sexual mayhem introduced to Brad
and Janet.

The film advocates for sexual
exploration regardless of outcome,
and to embrace your true self, as
long as you remember pleasure and
excess have consequences, as Frank
finds out.

"Tonight, my unconventional conventionists, you are to witness a new breakthrough. In biochemical research. And paradise is to be mine! You see, you are fortunate. For tonight is the night... that my beautiful creature is destined to be born."

**Dr Frank-N-Furter,** *The Rocky Horror Picture Show,* **1975**

# 55 MILLION

The total number of movie tickets for *The Rocky Horror Picture Show* that have been sold at cinemas since 1975. The film is currently No. 92 in the chart of most-watched cinema films worldwide, according to Box Office Mojo. Coincidentally, *Rocky*, the 1976 boxing film, is at No. 93.

FYI, Rocky Balboa's name is not based on *Rocky Horror*. The timing is close, but the names are a coincidence. Both take inspiration from the stereotype of a strong, muscular "Rocky" figure. *Rocky Horror*'s name is taken from the fact that Rocky's head is full of rocks!

"The live show has an energy that the movie doesn't have – it wasn't intentional, but the film is very slow. The movie is a very surreal, almost dream-like journey, the live show is far more rock and roll."

**Richard O'Brien,
Norwich Theatre, August 2023**

# "I have one thing to say and that's Dammit, Janet, I love you."

**Brad Majors, *The Rocky Horror Picture Show*, 1975**

# DAMMIT JANET

Composed by Richard O'Brien and Richard Hartley, the movie's second musical number 'Dammit Janet' is the film's most heartfelt, less zany moment. Sung inside the Denton Episcopal Church after Ralph and Betty Hapschatt's wedding, the song is performed by Brad and Janet after Brad proposes to Janet. "For as long as I live, people will be coming up to me and asking me to say, "Dammit, Janet. I love you,' Barry Bostwick told the *Virginian-Pilot* in July 2003.

The song was written during rehearsals for the stage show. "Brad and Janet needed their own song, so 'Dammit Janet' went in," Richard O'Brien told the *Guardian* in March 2013. "I think their sexual awakening is something we can all relate to, but it's not just a sexual rite of passage: when their car breaks down and they arrive at the castle, they're leaving the American dream and walking into an uncertain future."

"The only imperative from 20th Century Fox was that we include some American actors. That's why Barry Bostwick and Susan Sarandon play Brad and Janet."

**Richard O'Brien,**
*Guardian*, **March 2013**

# BRAD AND JANET'S LOVE STORY

In 2013, Richard O'Brien revealed that the two American lead actors who played Brad and Janet – Barry Bostwick and Susan Sarandon – were actually dating during filming. The couple's chemistry is clear in the song 'Dammit Janet'.

In 1983, Susan also revealed that she dated *Rocky Horror* fan, David Bowie, after working together on the British horror film *The Hunger*. "He's worth idolizing. He's extraordinary," she has said of her former "rock star" lover.

# THE CRITICS

When the movie came out in 1975, the critics were quick to consider it a piece of crap. It received almost universal condemnation from mainstream media. *Newsweek*, in 1978, were the meanest, calling the film "tasteless, plotless and pointless"; while *Variety* said, "Most of the jokes that might have seemed jolly fun on stage now appear obvious and even flat. The sparkle's gone."

Roger Ebert, the esteemed American film reviewer, saw its potential however, and gave the film 2½ stars (out of four) in his 1976 review:

"It's one of those movies you have to use a lot of hyphens to explain. A horror-rock-transvestite-camp-omnisexual-musical parody. *The Rocky Horror Picture Show* is not so much a movie as more of a long-running social phenomenon... and it invites the kind of laughter and audience participation that makes sense only if the performers are there on the stage, creating mutual karma."

# "You're lucky. He's lucky. I'm lucky. We're all lucky!"

**Magenta, *The Rocky Horror Picture Show*, 1975**

# EASTER EGGS

If you've ever wondered why films have "Easter eggs" – little hidden details in a shot waiting to be noticed by eagle-eyed fans – then look no further than *The Rocky Horror Picture Show*, it's where the term is rumoured to have originated. During filming, crew members would hide Easter* eggs around the set as part of an Easter egg hunt, to provide entertainment for the cast. Some eggs can be seen in the film – if you look closely enough.

*In true *Rocky Horror* form, the film was actually shot from October to December, encompassing both Halloween and Christmas – not Easter!

# ROCKY HORROR ETIQUETTE

As we all know, *Rocky Horror* isn't just a film — it is an experience that brings together people from all walks of life. For 50 years, audience participation, known as Rocky Horror Etiquette, has kept the film alive in cinemas, with fans dressing up as characters, shouting out lines and ad-libbed responses to dialogue, and singing along to the songs. There are hundreds, but these are some of the most well-known main call-outs and cues. What's your favourite?

## "ASSHOLE!"

Whenever Brad appears, or is introduced.

## "SLUT!"

When Janet is introduced or appears. If this is before she sleeps with Rocky, the response is met with its own response: "She's not a slut yet, give her a chance."

## "HE'S GOT NO FUCKING NECK!"

Whenever The Criminologist Charles Gray, the narrator, speaks. A joke about the actor Charles Gray's lack of a visible neck.

## "DON'T TOUCH IT, YOU'LL GO BLIND!"

When Janet sees the light-up sign that says "ENTER AT YOUR OWN RISK".

## "LET'S DO THE TIME WARP AGAIN!"

When the song 'Time Warp' starts.

## "SAY IT!!!"

When Frank-N-Furter sings "I see you shiver with antici... pation!" The audience finishes the phrase with this punchline before Frank can say it.

## "BULLWINKLE!"

When Frank says "Rocky!" for the first time.

"It thrills me that my grandchildren may see their grandmother in her half-slip and bra, seducing a monster."

**Susan Sarandon, *Chicago Tribune*, December 1993**

# SUSAN SARANDON

While Tim Curry went on to great fame and acclaim after 1975, so too did his co-star Susan Sarandon who played Janet Weiss. *Rocky Horror* was her first gig in a musical, but soon she was being nominated for Academy Awards, and won, for her role in *Dead Man Walking* (1995). Today, she is perhaps best known as one-half of *Thelma & Louise*, the 1991 hit that made her a household name in America. Susan landed the role of Janet by singing 'Happy Birthday' at her audition to prove she could sing.

Upon the release of the movie's soundtrack in 1975, it sold more than one million copies and remained on the Billboard US chart for more than a year.

Today, the soundtrack on Spotify has amassed tens of millions of streams, with 'Time Warp' having more than 85 million listens in total. What's your favourite track?

# Song List

1. 'Science Fiction/Double Feature'
   – Magenta

2. 'Dammit Janet' – Brad, Janet

3. 'Over at the Frankenstein Place'
   – Brad, Janet, Riff-Raff

4. 'Time Warp' – Riff Raff, Magenta,
   Columbia, The Criminologist

5. 'Sweet Transvestite' – Frank-N-Furter

6. 'I Can Make You a Man' – Frank-N-Furter

7. 'Hot Patootie – Bless My Soul' – Eddie

8. 'Touch-a, Touch-a, Touch-a, Touch Me'
   – Janet, Magenta, Columbia

9. 'Eddie's Teddy' – Dr Scott, Columbia,
   The Transylvanians

10. 'Planet Schmanet, Janet' – Frank-N-Furter

11. 'Rose Tint My World' – Columbia, Rocky,
    Janet, Brad

12. 'Don't Dream It, Be It' – Frank-N-Furter

13. 'Wild and Untamed Thing'
    – Frank-N-Furter

14. 'I'm Going Home' – Frank-N-Furter

15. 'Super Heroes' – Brad, Janet, Narrator

# 1 APRIL 1976

The date of the first ever midnight screening of *The Rocky Horror Picture Show*, a film revered as the "ultimate midnight movie". April Fool's Day, naturally!

The venue was the Waverly Theatre, New York, at 323 Sixth Avenue/West 3rd Street. Midnight screenings have become a standardised ritual for cinema screenings all over the world, along with audience participation and "prop bags". "It was a great pleasure for me when I finally found out that *Rocky Horror* was gaining popularity on the midnight circuit," Richard O'Brien said in 1979. "I always thought I would have to take the play back to New York to give it a second chance. Now it doesn't need one."

# 54 WEEKS STRAIGHT

The movie's reputation for being the longest continually running film in cinema history did not stop during the global lockdown of 2020 and 2021. Not even COVID-19 could tame this wild thing!

The Clinton Street Theatre in Portland, Oregon, screened the movie every Saturday night at 9pm to an empty house for 54 weeks, while it was closed. "I watched it alone. I watched it during the snowstorm," Nathan Williams, the cinema's owner told Movie web in August 2021.

"I was in a position to keep a flame burning, to keep a torch lit. I'm just a guy holding a torch for the city of Portland, for all the weirdos, for all the people who don't have a safe place to call home, we're home. It's just kind of a silly little thing, but it was still a sense of hope. This is what normal is. Normal is we play *Rocky Horror* on a Saturday night, and that's what's happening."

"When someone suggested we do *Rocky* as a film I just went along for the ride. I said, 'Oh yeah, sure'. I was very casual about the whole thing. It seemed quite surreal to me. I never went home and said, 'Wow! We're going to make a movie!' I've thought about it since though and said, 'Wow! We *made* a movie!'"

**Richard O'Brien, Blu-Ray.com, 2011**

# ASTOUNDING

After reading the script for the first time and clocking its run time – just over 40 minutes – song composer Richard Hartley told Rocky Horror creator Richard O'Brien that the show was too short and would need to be stretched out. He suggested adding a new song.

Written in one night, and borrowing inspiration for its first line – "It's astounding" – from a magazine sitting on Richard's kitchen table, *Astounding Science Fiction* (originally printed in October 1953), the 'Time Warp' is undoubtedly *Rocky Horror*'s most famous song. Inspired by *Rocky Horror*, rock singer Freddie Mercury used the cover of *Astounding Science Fiction* for Queen's 1977 *News of the World* album cover, a record that features 'We Are The Champions' and 'We Will Rock You'.

# PIZZA DELIVERY

Despite only being (alive) in the movie for four minutes, Meatloaf's performance of pizza delivery boy Eddie is as big and bold and brilliant as Meat Loaf was himself. After having donated part of his brain to Frank's "Rocky" creation, Eddie is then frozen alive. He pops out of the deep freeze at around the 40-minute mark to sing 'Hot Patootie – Bless My Soul', the movie's big 1950s rock number. Incredibly, Meat Loaf nailed this performance in one take. In 1977, Meat Loaf's *Bat Out of Hell* album coincided with the growing popularity of *The Rocky Horror Picture Show* and went on to sell 45 million copies worldwide.

"They come to me on the part of 'Hot Patootie', and Richard O'Brien is here at these rehearsals... he said 'on this song you'll never be able to get all the words in. ... I wrote it and I can't sing all the words.' I looked at him and said, 'I can sing all the words,' Nobody could ever get in and just make those words fly through it. I just love telling people 'I can do that' and then being able to do it."

Meat Loaf, Gold Radio, September 2023

After Meatloaf's heavyweight performance in David Fincher's *Fight Club* (1999), a popular audience call back following the revelation of Eddie's corpse became,

**"HIS NAME WAS ROBERT PAULSON! HIS NAME WAS ROBERT PAULSON!"**

"The strange thing is that *Rocky* is a parody of the cinema for stage so actually putting it on film was a bit disorienting. Were we reverting to the original, the thing that was being parodied? Or was it a comment upon a comment upon a comment?"

**Richard O'Brien,
Blu-Ray.com, 2011**

"I always had faith in the originality of the film and felt it would ultimately find its audience, but the early signs weren't good. The fact that it was such an unusual film and that it was devoid of conventional movie stars didn't help. The fashion of the day was for realist films and this was... *something else.* The mainstream audience only saw the surface, and they turned away; but the late-night audience picked up on what was under that surface – and it spoke to them."

Jim Sharman, RHPS Official Fan Club, August 2008

# ROCKY VIRGINS

Those who haven't bathed in the camp, creamy glory of The *Rocky Horror Picture Show* – Virgins, as we call them – should visit rockyhorror.co.uk and learn the "Virgin Survival Guide" of call-outs, dress, etiquette, dance moves and chant-alongs.

At most midnight screenings of the movie, Virgins have to endure/enjoy a Virgin Initiation, a ritual that often sees them marked with a large V on the forehead in red lipstick. Don't worry, it doesn't hurt. Unless you want it to.

# "I can't really relate to the film very well. I still feel sick when I see it."

**Tim Curry, *Interview*, 1976**

# 35 MILLION

The number of theatre goers who have seen the *Rocky Horror* stage show since its first public outing in 1973.

The stage show has also been translated into 20 languages and performed in 30 countries. Performances of 'Zeitsprung' ('Time Warp') is particularly good for the soul.

Dr Scott: Janet!

Janet: Dr Scott!

Brad: Janet!

Janet: Brad!

Frank: Rocky!

*[Rocky looks over to Frank]*

Dr Scott: Janet!

Janet: Dr Scott!

Brad: Janet!

Janet: Brad!

Frank: Rocky!

*[Rocky looks over to Frank]*

Dr Scott: Janet!

Janet: Dr Scott!

Brad: Janet!

Janet: Brad!

Frank: Rocky!

*[Rocky looks over to Frank]*

One of the most hilarious – and iconic – exchanges in the movie is in the third act, after Brad finds out that his fiancée Janet and Rocky have had, no doubt, rather hot monster sex.

The scene doesn't really translate in book form, but we couldn't not include it – it's a classic.

# WELCOME TO DENTON – THE HOME OF HAPPINESS

In 1972, while Richard O'Brien was writing the stage play, it was originally titled *They Came From Denton High*, a title borrowed from Richard's love of sci-fi B-movies, such as *It Came from Outer Space*. The title changed after Richard showed the musical director Jim Sharman. "I basically suggested the title of *Rocky Horror Show* to Richard on the simple principle that it's a rock and roll horror show, why don't we just call it what it is?" he told the *L.A. Times* in November 2015.

In the movie, Denton is depicted as a town in northeast Ohio, even though there is no Denton in Ohio (though there are 12 towns in America called Denton).

"Frank's a drama queen, really. He's a hedonistic, self-indulgent voluptuary, and that's his downfall. He's ego-driven and I was going to say, *a bit like my mother*."

**Richard O'Brien, *The Times*, August 2009**

# CHAPTER THREE

# THRILL ME, CHILL ME, FULFIL ME

# "Oh, slowly, slowly! It's too nice a job to rush!"

**Columbia, *The Rocky Horror Picture Show*, 1975**

"This sonic transducer...
it is, I suppose, some kind
of audio-vibratory-physio-
molecular transport device?
A device which is capable of
breaking down solid matter
and projecting it through
space... and, who knows,
perhaps even time itself!"

**Dr Scott, *The Rocky Horror
Picture Show*, 1975**

The sonic transducer is just one of several toys
Frank owns; others include a Sonic Oscillator,
Reactor Power Input, Triple Contact Electro
Magnet and Medusa.

# "Buy an umbrella, you cheap bitch!"

This now-legendary heckle was one of the first ad-libbed call-outs shouted at the screen during the movie's 20-month midnight screening run at the Waverly Theatre, New York, sometime in September 1976.

According to various sources, the first call-out was "Buy an umbrella, you cheap bitch!", hollered at Janet when she puts a newspaper over her head during the movie's opening thunderstorm. The response was shouted by Louis Farese, Jr., a schoolteacher who attended the Waverly with friends Theresa Krakauskas and Amy Lazarus. "We were just trying to have a good time," Lazarus said, unknowingly starting a trend that would last half a century... and beyond!

# THE DANCE

The 'Time Warp' dance – O'Brien's most famous creation's famous creation – is one of the most popular songs played at Halloween and is the major audience participation point during screenings. "I could listen to that song on repeat for hours," the Hollywood actor Jack Black has said of the song. "I would call that the centrepiece of the masterpiece of the music of the movie."

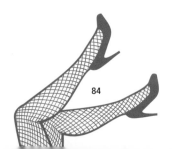

"The dance was just because dance songs are always so silly – do the Twist, the Hucklebuck, the Madison, the Loco-motion, the Funky Chicken, they went on forever. The Time Warp was to laugh at and enjoy the dance crazes."

**Richard O'Brien,**
*Radio Times*, **June 2023**

# "Say, do any of you guys know how to Madison?"

**Brad Majors,**
***The Rocky Horror Picture Show,***
**1975**

Brad's line about the "Madison" refers to a popular country-and-western dance that was popular in America from the 1960s.

It shows what a square he is, asking for a dance that is more traditional and conventional in nature, after having been terrified by the aliens' 'Time Warp'.

# REMEMBER YOUR PROP BAG

For decades, no midnight screening of the movie has been complete without audience "Prop Bags". Often supplied by the cinema themselves, and sometimes prepared by fan clubs or friendship groups, the prop bags are filled with items to be used at particular times during the show and movie.

There's even the Toast Tradition. This involves audiences throwing toast at the screen when Frank says, "A toast!" during dinner (eating Eddie).

Other popular interactive traditions involve throwing rice during the Hapschatt wedding scene, and using newspapers as shields for when Brad and Janet are caught in the storm.

## Here's a quick list of some props:

* **Water pistols** (to simulate rain)

* **Candles** (to light, when Janet says, "There's a light on over at Frankenstein Place.")

* **Rubber gloves** (to snap, when Frank unveils Rocky)

* **Confetti** (to throw, when Frank and Rocky head to the bedroom)

* **Toilet paper** (to throw, when Dr Scott exclaims "Great Scott!")

* **Deck of cards** (to throw, when Frank sings 'I'm Going Home')

"*Rocky* is a place for the marginalized. I see *Rocky*, now, as a rainbow event. I'm not a flag waver. But the flag I would stand by is the rainbow flag. And I think *Rocky* is important in that respect."

Richard O'Brien,
*Big Issue*, June 2023

# GENDER QUESTIONING

As quickly as the film started to become a cult concern, it was adopted by the queer community as an icon of LGBTQIA+ beliefs.

The film's themes of gender fluidity and sexuality made it a landmark for the community's representation in cinema. Frank-N-Furter's mix of masculinity and femininity challenged traditional gender roles decades before mainstream media embraced gender diversity. Richard O'Brien based Frank's gender fluidity on himself, as Richard himself identifies as "70 per cent male, 30 per cent female" (BBC, March 2013).

# "You've arrived on a rather special night. It's one of the master's affairs."

**Riff-Raff, *The Rocky Horror Picture Show*, 1975**

In 2016, a $20 million TV remake of *The Rocky Horror Picture Show* was made by Fox called *Let's Do the Time Warp Again.* The movie was a faithful adaptation and tribute to the original story, but sanitized for American teen audiences, removing much of the campness and energy that makes the original feel unique.

The movie was made by the creator of the *High School Musical* trilogy, Kenny Ortega, and starred Laverne Cox as Dr Frank-N-Furter and Nickelodeon starlet Victoria Justice as Janet. Pop star Adam Lambert pops in to play Eddie, which is a lot of fun.

While Richard O'Brien owns the rights to the stage show, entertainment giant Disney now owns the rights to *The Rocky Horror Picture Show* after their takeover of 20th Century Fox in 2019.

After the deal, Disney began removing older film reels and stock from theatres to be put into archival vaults.

However, *The Rocky Horror Picture Show* was permitted to continue its traditional midnight screenings at theatres with non-digital film projectors.

"My God! I can't stand any more of this! First you spurn me for Eddie, and then you throw him off like an old overcoat for Rocky! You chew people up and then you spit them out again! I loved you... do you hear me? I loved you! And what did it get me? Yeah, I'll tell you: a big nothing! You're like a sponge, you take, take, take, and drain others of their love and emotion! Yeah, well, I've had enough! You're gonna choose between me and Rocky, so named cause of the rocks in his head!"

Columbia, *The Rocky Horror Picture Show*, 1975

# $1,600

The costume budget for the *entire* movie! The corsets alone, worn by Frank and Columbia, cost $200!

Despite the lack of funds, costume designer Sue Blane went on to effectively invent the punk aesthetic that defined the late 1970s. "With such a small budget, everything *had* to be junk," Sue Blane said, in 1979, of the film's lack of resources.

"I went to a sold-out midnight screening one time in 1978 in New York with bunch of friends, and I tell the manager that I'm in the movie, but they didn't believe me! They finally believed me, and said, 'You better be Meat Loaf, 'cause we're sitting you at the front!' They sat me next to these two people who said they had seen the film 220 times in a row, and who were snorting cocaine throughout the movie getting really into it. The fans, the screenings, everything, I mean it was total insanity."

**Meat Loaf, *Late Night With David Letterman*, 1982**

"Listed, gloomy and semi-derelict, with its owner living abroad, it was perfect for us."

**Jim Sharman, *L.A. Times*, November 2015**

Between October and December 1974, the movie was shot on location at Oakley Court, Windsor, a large gothic Victorian mansion estate that doubled wonderfully as Frankenstein Place. Prior to filming, the house, built in 1859, had been used in many Hammer Horror films. Today, the mansion has been restored and is a luxury hotel.

# "That's a rather tender subject. Another slice, anyone?"

**Dr Frank-N-Furter, *The Rocky Horror Picture Show*, 1975**

"The show allows the kids to dress up. It's a major breakthrough. Thanks to *Rocky Horror* a guy can put on fishnets and strut his stuff and feel okay."

Richard O'Brien, *Rocky Horror Picture Show Official Magazine* 1979

Designed by costume designer Sue Blane, Frank's corset-and-heels look was inspired by London's then-burgeoning glam (and glitter) rock scene. Many androgynous rock artists such as David Bowie, Marc Bolan, Freddie Mercury and Elton John then borrowed inspiration for their looks from the movie. According to Patrica Quinn, who plays Magenta, the main reason King Charles has never seen the film is due to the outrageous costumes. "I invited him to see the show but he said he couldn't really go because of the fishnets and suspenders!" Quinn told the BBC, August 2023.

"It had nothing to do with shocking people. I wrote *Rocky* for me. I didn't write it with an audience in mind or for it to be a hit. When we transferred to the Classic Cinema from The Pheasantry, I came out of the first night and Michael White, our producer, said: 'I think we've got a hit, Richard!' And I said: 'Have we?' And I got in the car and went home."

Richard O'Brien, *Pink News*, November 2011

In 2020, a week before the 2020 US presidential election between Republican Donald Trump and Democrat Joe Biden, the rock band Tenacious D, fronted by *Rocky* fan Jack Black, recorded a politically motivated video version of 'Time Warp', for the Rock the Vote campaign, renamed "Rock-y the Vote"! A number of politicians and celebrities, including Sarah Silverman, Phoebe Bridgers, Jamie Lee Curtis, Eric Andre, Elizabeth Warren and Susan Sarandon got involved. For his version, Jack asked participants to change the song's lyric to be "it's just a jump to the left, and *not* a step to the right", encouraging viewers to vote for the Democratic Party. The video got more than five million views. The Democrats won!

# $600

The total budget that set designer Brian Thompson had for the whole movie – just $600!  Luckily, the filming location for Frank's castle, Oakley Court, had been used for several Hammer Horror movies, and so many of the props seen in the film – such as the tank and the dummy used in Rocky's birth sequence – were simply repurposed as leftovers from films such as *The Revenge of Frankenstein*, *The Man in Black*, *The Lady Craved Excitement*, *The Brides of Dracula*, *The Reptile* and *The Plague of the Zombies* – movies that inspired Richard O'Brien to write the stage show in the first place!

Janet Weiss: "What have you done to Brad?"

Dr Frank-N-Furter: "Nothing. Why, do you think I should?"

**Janet Weiss & Dr Frank-N-Furter,**
***The Rocky Horror Picture Show,***
**1975**

# CHAPTER FOUR

## HOT PATOOTIES

# FOUR HOURS

The time it took Tim Curry to apply his Frank make-up every single day of the five-week shoot. After the first week, and due to severe time constraints during filming and lack of a budget, Tim learnt how to apply the make-up himself.

# 8,239

The number of participants who danced together to break the world record for "Most Dancers Doing the 'Time Warp'".

The achievement was accomplished in West Hollywood, California on Halloween 2010, to celebrate the 35th anniversary of the film. Guinness World Records were there to confirm the record as official.

In 1974, at the American debut of the stage show at the Roxy Theatre in LA, Meat Loaf attended a performance. There, he met Elvis Presley, a huge *Rocky Horror* fan. As everyone knows, the character of Eddie was originally inspired by Elvis Presley.

"Elvis came to see the stage version of *The Rocky Horror Picture Show* at The Roxy. He wanted to meet me and Tim Curry. He asked, "I hear that everybody else had been impersonating me when they did the character of 'Eddie' but you didn't." I said, 'There's no point in me imitating you because it would be impossible.' That's all I said to him."

**Meat Loaf, *Goldmine*, January 2022**

In 2005, just as the movie celebrated its 30th birthday, BBC Radio 2 asked the nation to vote for its favourite musical. The nation spoke, and *Rocky* was present, coming in at No. 8.

1. *Les Misérables*
2. *Phantom Of The Opera*
3. *Seven Brides For Seven Brothers*
4. *The King And I*
5. *Sunset Boulevard*
6. *Evita*
7. *Chess*
8. *The Rocky Horror Show*
9. *Follies*
10. *Hair*

Janet actress Susan Sarandon contracted pneumonia while filming the movie.

The set was notoriously cold as it was November, and Susan had to spend most of the first act of the film dressed only in a bra and slip, and getting wet from the thunderstorm and the pool scene for the shooting of the song 'Wild and Untamed Thing'. The derelict Oakley Court also barely had a roof, and it rained for most of the filming.

After the shoot, Susan returned to LA and promptly collapsed. "It was mentally and physically not a healthy thing that I did," she has said.

"Up until very recently, I've argued that *Rocky* is just a piece of silly nonsense. But the religious right has started becoming vocal and horrible. Nationalism in America is terrifying. The lack of kindness towards the LGBT+ community is astonishing. And we're taking steps backwards. So, I think maybe *Rocky* is becoming more important by default."

**Richard O'Brien, *Big Issue*, June 2023**

Richard O' Brien's enduring memory of the opening night of the first ever stage show production in 1973 to just 63 people:

**"There was a big electrical storm and Vincent Price was sitting in the audience under the skylight. The lightning flashed and lit him up. I thought: 'Fuck me, that's a good omen!' The theatre was packed and sweaty. There wasn't a spare inch. We had one microphone hanging down from the ceiling, and it would swing past the audience's heads."**

(*Guardian*, November 2020)

Richard's idol, Vincent Price, a horror-movie star after his leading role in Hammer's 1953 *House of Wax*, was present and loved the show. The part of the Criminologist/narrator was written with Vincent Price in mind, and he was originally offered the part.

# ROCKY INSPO

Fans of the movie will know that many of the lyrics in the movie's songs refer back to the science-fiction and horror films that Richard O'Brien loved to watch as a child – and adult! If you're looking to take your *Rocky* inspiration to the next level, go sniff out these iconic influences:

* *Doctor X* (1932)
* *King Kong* (1933)
* *The Invisible Man* (1933)
* *Flash Gordon* (1936)
* *The Day the Earth Stood Still* (1951)
* *When Worlds Collide* (1951)
* *It Came from Outer Space* (1953)
* *Tarantula* (1955)
* *Forbidden Planet* (1956)
* *Curse of the Demon* (1957)
* *The Day of the Triffids* (1962)

# OF ALL TIME

In January 2017, America's most influential film and TV magazine *Rolling Stone* asked its two million readers what the best movie musical of all time was. You know the answer! Yes, Rocky Horror came No. 1 in the poll, beating classics such as *The Blues Brothers*, *Grease*, *West Side Story* and even *Singin' in the Rain*.

**"No film – musical, or otherwise – has spawned the cult following *Rocky Horror Picture Show* has since its release. Fans continue to dress up and attend packed, interactive screenings across the world, singing along to the rock-leaning tunes attached to the deliciously weird sci-fi horror tale."**

***Rolling Stone*, January 2017**

On the opening night of the first performance of the *Rocky Horror Show*, UK newspaper reviewer Michael Billington was there in the 63-seat audience of the Royal Court Theatre.

He was one of many reviewers who gave *Rocky Horror,* and its performers, two thumbs up.

He wrote: *"It achieves the rare feat of being witty and erotic at the same time."* (*Guardian*, June 1973)

# "It's not easy having a good time! Even smiling makes my face ache!"

**Dr Frank-N-Furter, *The Rocky Horror Picture Show*, 1975**

# MUSCLEMAN

Tim Curry was the stand out star of both the original stage show and the movie. However, Tim getting the part was more accident than design. He literally bumped into Richard O'Brien. "I saw Richard O'Brien in the street outside a gym off Baker Street, and went up to him," Tim told *NEA* in December 1992. "He said he'd just been to the gym to see if he could find a muscleman who could sing for the role of Rocky. He gave me the script, and told me to talk to Jim Sharman. I read the script and thought, 'Boy, if this works, it's going to be a smash.'"

# SHOOTS OF CHANGE

In London in the early 1970s, Richard O'Brien was an out-of-work actor. He started writing the *Rocky Horror Show* to keep himself busy on winter evenings.

In his childhood he had developed a passion for science-fiction and horror B-movies, and he used his story of *Rocky* to combine elements from both into a camp, kitsch and schlocky-horror tale. The element of transvestism only came much later on in rehearsals.

"*Rocky Horror* was probably not the first example of gender-bending on film, but it was the most in-your-face," O'Brien said told the *Guardian* in March 2013.

"He's kind of an extremist, Frank. His life is devoted to... extremity. He says he's a transvestite transexual, whatever that means. I don't play him as a transexual. But he's a fairly complex guy. He just takes anything he can get. He's not fussy, really. Though I think he's something of a wham-bam-thank-you-ma'am."

**Tim Curry, *L.A. Times*, March 1974**

# 1:09.44

The precise time at which one of the film's most popular – and unexpected! – moments happens. It is the revelation of Eddie's butchered corpse hidden beneath the table during the notorious dinner scene. When Frank dramatically exposes the body, the dinner guests squeal in horror.

Director Jim Sharman deliberately kept this twist a secret from most of the cast, with only Tim Curry, Richard O'Brien and Meat Loaf aware – Meat Loaf, of course, had to play the corpse. As a result, the cast's stunned reactions are completely real!

# 14 SEPTEMBER 1986

The first night the Sins O' The Flesh cast performed alongside *The Rocky Horror Picture Show* at the Nuart Theatre, Santa Monica, California.

They have performed every Saturday night at midnight ever since. That's nearly 40 years! They are the longest performing *Rocky Horror* cast in history. How long can they keep it up?

# DRAG ALL DAY

Drag is, today, one of the most influential forms of entertainment in TV and film, rising to prominence through *RuPaul's Drag Race*, a reality show and drag competition.

Over the years, many of the world's greatest drag performers, such as RuPaul, Lady Bunny, Trixie Mattel, Sasha Colby and Bianca del Rio, have praised *The Rocky Horror Picture Show* for its gender-fluidity and putting transvestism front and centre. "This film is a musical that has brought freaks together from all over the world and it stands the test of time. It's a film that asks you to respond to it," Sharon Needles said introducing the movie at RuPaul's DragCon 2015. Too right, sister!

*Rocky Horror* is a Halloween staple, with special screenings and stage performances increasing significantly every October. In the UK, most independent cinemas and multiplexes offer tickets for at least one midnight screening.

The film has been associated with 31 October since 1976, when fans would go dressed up as their favourite *Rocky Horror* characters to Halloween parties and then midnight screenings. Rocky's golden speedos, or Frank corsets and fishnets are, of course, the most popular Halloween costumes.

"Rocky Horror is just Frankenstein with a twist. Except there's no twisting — it's rock'n'roll. Richard and I listened to the same records when we were growing up, so we just put all the things we loved in. You can hear the influences: a bit of Chuck Berry, and a bit of Rolling Stones in 'Sweet Transvestite.'"

**Richard Hartley,**
***Guardian*, March 2013**

# MAKE-UP GENIUS

The genius behind the characters' incredible make-up designs were the vision of Pierre La Roche, a hair and make-up consultant on the movie who was brought in to soften the stage show look for the big screen.

In the 1970s, Pierre was famous for creating the iconic "forehead lightning bolt" design on Bowie's Ziggy Stardust character as well as Bowie's "Aladdin Sane" face-paint. He was also the Rolling Stones' make-up artist when they were on tour. Yes, they had one.

# DON'T DREAM IT...

# BE IT!